In *Be Still & Know*, Brian Cosby offers the opportunity to practice what too many believers have neglected: meditation on the character of God. Leading us through God's attributes with careful Biblical exegesis combined with experienced pastoral sensitivities, Cosby employs a five-fold method of unfolding the Biblical and practical beauty of the Lord in His self-revealed attributes. The end result is a devotional journey into a daily life of meditation on God Himself that leaves the reader transformed by the glory of the Lord. Take and read! Take and meditate! Your mind and heart will be the better for it!

—**Michael A. Milton**, Chancellor and James M. Baird Jr. Professor of Pastoral Theology, Reformed Theological Seminary, and author of *Small Things, Big Things*

The first question we ask when reading Scripture should not be, "What can the Bible do for me?" The better question is, "What does the Bible teach me about God?" Knowing God is the key to spiritual progress and Brian Cosby has written a masterful book designed to help us grow. Whether for personal devotion or group Bible study, *Be Still & Know* will prove an outstanding introduction to the character of God. For some, this book will be revolutionary – releasing them from the cycle of self-centered obsession to God-glorifying worship.

—**Derek W. H. Thomas**, John E. Richards Professor of Theology, RTS Jackson, Minister of Teaching, First Presbyterian Church, Jackson, Editorial Director, Alliance of Confessing Evangelicals, and author of *Making the Most of Your Devotional Life*

In his book, *Be Still & Know*, Brian Cosby comes alongside the reader and gently introduces him/her to the character of God. Written in a meditation format, Cosby's work is based on Scripture. At the beginning of each meditation, he suggests a Scripture reading, and a prayer for the reader to pray. After the Bible-based meditation, Cosby continues to invite the reader to participate with questions for personal reflection, and a "Digging Deeper" section. I highly recommend this work by this young theologian. I believe it will encourage, inspire, teach, and offer hope for all those who read it.

—**Denise George**, speaker, teacher, and author of 25 books, including *Come to the Quiet* and *Planting Trust, Knowing Peace*

Be Still & Know

Be Still & Know

Meditations on the Character of God

Brian H. Cosby

WestBow
PRESS
A DIVISION OF THOMAS NELSON

WestBow Press books may be ordered through booksellers or by contacting:

WestBow Press
A Division of Thomas Nelson
1663 Liberty Drive
Bloomington, IN 47403
www.westbowpress.com
1-(866) 928-1240

Because of the dynamic nature of the Internet, any Web addresses or links contained in this book may have changed since publication and may no longer be valid. The views expressed in this work are solely those of the author and do not necessarily reflect the views of the publisher, and the publisher hereby disclaims any responsibility for them.

Any people depicted in stock imagery provided by Thinkstock are models, and such images are being used for illustrative purposes only.

Certain stock imagery © Thinkstock.

ISBN: 978-1-4497-1091-0 (sc)
ISBN: 978-1-4497-1090-3 (e)

Library of Congress Control Number: 2010943529

Printed in the United States of America

WestBow Press rev. date: 1/13/2011

Contents

Foreword

The prophet Jeremiah wrote:

> Let not the wise man boast in his wisdom, let not
> the mighty man boast in his might, let not the rich
> man boast in his riches, but let him who boasts
> boast in this, that he understands and knows me,
> that I am the LORD who practices steadfast love,
> justice, and righteousness in the earth. For in these
> things I delight, declares the LORD (Jer. 9:23-24).

There is a crisis of commitment and spiritual maturity among Christians in the church today, largely because there is so little emphasis and pursuit of understanding and knowing God as He has revealed Himself in the Scriptures. Jesus prayed, "Sanctify them in the truth, your word is truth" (Jn. 17:17). The pursuit of knowing God through His Word will result in continual personal transformation and growing affection for Him, but sadly many believers have not had the opportunity to learn or observe how this is done. For this reason, it is with great enthusiasm that I recommend to you *Be Still & Know* by Brian Cosby.

Brian's focus on knowing God is refreshingly biblical, simple, and yet profound in our day. He calls the disciple of Christ to go beyond a superficial understanding of God and to take the time to focus deeply on many of His key attributes. The reader will find the five practical directional signs applied to the study of each attribute a very effective means to personally discovering and encountering the glory of God. The true power of this study is the emphasis on experiencing each quality of God ultimately through the person and work of Jesus Christ, and what He did for believers in the gospel.

As a senior pastor, I have had the privilege of working with Brian as a friend and colleague on the staff at our church. The material in this helpful book has been borne from his careful study of God's Word, and growth in the grace and communion of Jesus Christ. As Brian has lived and taught these truths, I've observed a surprising level of spiritual maturity produced in many of his students. I'm convinced every Christian will be challenged and encouraged to fall more deeply in love with God through this gospel-centered and practical treatment of His attributes.

Doug Griffith
Senior Pastor
Carriage Lane Presbyterian Church
Peachtree City, Georgia

Preface

The purpose of this book is to guide you, the reader, in meditating on God's perfect character and attributes so that your mind will be transformed, your affections kindled, and your faith nourished by his grace. Many competing distractions attempt to steal your time and fill your schedule so that you are tempted by sheer busyness from taking time to meditate on him. But God calls us to "be still and know that he is God" (Ps. 46:10). Who is God and how are we to "be still" before him? The answer to those questions is the aim of this book.

This book was not originally my idea. Several people in my church—Carriage Lane Presbyterian Church in Peachtree City, Georgia—asked me to write it. I am indebted to the men and women with whom I serve and minister. I am especially grateful to my wife, Ashley, for her constant encouragement, wisdom, and love. She was the spark that set this book in motion.

It is my hope that you will use this guide and resource to focus your thoughts and channel your love on the God who is. May his perfect character instill greater desire and love for him and may the gospel of Jesus Christ be evident as it is expressed from God's manifold attributes. Indeed,

To him who is able to keep you from stumbling and to present you blameless before the presence of his glory with great joy, to the only God, our Savior, through Jesus Christ our Lord, be glory, majesty, dominion, and authority, before all time and now and forever. Amen (Jude 24-25).

Brian H. Cosby
Advent, 2010

Introduction:
Meditating on God's Character

Meditating on God's Word is one of the most rewarding and faith-sustaining disciplines in the Christian life. It ushers the believer into greater communion with God and satisfies the longing soul. Meditation is a lingering over, a chewing on, and a wrestling with God's Word until—like Jacob wrestling with the angel—you are blessed by its promises and nourished by its truth.

The purpose of this book is to provide you with meditations on God's character and attributes so that you will grow in both a greater knowledge and love of the Rock of your salvation. While there are many devotionals in the marketplace offering guidance into the treasures of God's Word, *Be Still & Know* specifically reflects on God's manifold perfections as a means through which he—by his Spirit—graciously transforms our minds, changes our hearts, and molds us into the image of his Son, Jesus Christ.

Another purpose of this book is to provide a door through which you may enter into a deeper relationship with God by offering the following five sections for each attribute:

> **Scripture Meditation**
> **Prayer**
> **In Biblical Perspective**
> **Reflection Questions**
> **Digging Deeper**

These are meant to be practical directional signs, pointing to the true and living God and his gracious work of drawing sinners into a living and active fellowship with him.

In each meditation, the full Scripture passage itself is given so that you may conveniently reference the text as you go along in your study and reflection upon God's character. It is recommended, however, to have your own copy of God's Word available so as to look up various passages referenced or to read the surrounding context. It is also recommended that you read through the passage slowly and intentionally, thinking about each word and the overall message. In fact, it would be best to read it out loud several times through.

Praying at the start of each meditation is meant to set your mind afresh on this delight and privilege. It is taken from the passage and is to remind you of God's absolute power, wisdom, and love and your absolute dependence upon him as your heavenly Father. It is also to ask God to give you a teachable and soft heart so as to be instructed, encouraged, challenged, and changed. Prayer is possible only through the mediation of Jesus Christ. As the writer of Hebrews exhorts:

> *Since we have confidence to enter the holy places*
> *by the blood of Jesus, by the new and living way*

that he opened for us through the curtain, that is,
through his flesh, and since we have a great priest
over the house of God, let us draw near with a true
heart in full assurance of faith (Heb. 10:19-22).

Furthermore, we are to pray *expectantly*, with full assurance of our position and righteous standing before God. Because our sin has been credited—*imputed*—to Christ's account and his righteousness credited to our account by faith alone, we have been declared "not guilty" before a holy and just God. This, of course, is the doctrine of justification by faith alone. We can, therefore, enter into God's presence with prayers of praise, confession, intercession, thanksgiving, and supplication.

The section entitled "In Biblical Perspective" simply explains some of the historical, biblical, and theological background of the attribute of God under study and guides your thoughts on the truths of that attribute. It will also seek to show how each attribute is related to the gospel of Jesus Christ.

Sadly, many Christians today will read their Bible without making a connection to the gospel. The effect is either moralism (an attempt to *earn* merit or righteousness before God by works) or confusion over the overall purpose of the biblical text. The gospel, however, is the good news that, while you are far more sinful than you would ever imagine, you are—through faith alone in Christ alone—more accepted and loved than you would ever dream or hope.

Jesus himself explained that all of Scripture points to him and his life-work. While he was walking on the road to Emmaus after his resurrection, he tells his traveling companions that all of Scripture points to him. Luke records, "And beginning with Moses and all the Prophets, he interpreted to them in all the

Scriptures the things concerning himself" (Lk. 24:27). The apostle Paul writes in 2 Corinthians 1:20, that "all the promises of God find their Yes in him." Indeed, the Word of God is chiefly about the *Word* of God (Jn. 1:1), Jesus Christ.

Reflection Questions are provided with each chapter to help you think through and reflect on how the truth of God's character influences and directs your daily life. This is meant to be a very practical section in which probing questions are asked of your habits, thoughts, emotions, and actions. Space is also provided for you to write your thoughts down so as to remember them later or share them with others. To be sure, this will take some discipline, time, and honesty as you think through the implications of God's attributes and how Christ is made perfect in your weakness (2 Cor. 12:9).

The final section in each chapter, Digging Deeper, provides further Scripture passages, questions, thoughts, quotations, and other resources on each characteristic of God. If you find yourself especially encouraged by a certain attribute of God, then you may find this section particularly helpful.

It is important to remember that we are to *meditate* on God in his Word. The Psalmist writes that the believer is blessed when "his delight is in the law of the LORD and on his law he meditates day and night" (Ps. 1:2). He goes on to say that he "is like a tree planted by streams of water that yields its fruit in its season and its leaf does not wither" (v. 3). In other words, God is in the business of planting us and growing us into oaks of righteousness (Is. 61:3) through meditation on his Word. In addition, meditation will lead to the increase of spiritual fruit—love, joy, peace, patience, kindness, goodness, faithfulness, gentleness, and self control (Gal. 5:22-23).

During the sixteenth century, Martin Luther began what we now call the Protestant Reformation—a movement that eventually led to a break from the Roman Catholic Church. Luther debated many people over the nature of salvation, faith, and the authority of the church. One of those people was a man named Erasmus, who believed that humans had complete moral freedom to choose God on their own. Luther responded in a letter to Erasmus by saying, "Your thoughts concerning God are too human."[1]

Perhaps as you pick up this book, you find that your thoughts on God are far too human. Maybe you have succumbed, like many of us, to the temptation to believe that we are entitled to blessings from God. The truth is that nobody has arrived in a complete understanding of who God is in his fullness. Paul writes, however, that we are "stewards of the mysteries of God" (1 Cor. 4:1). We have been given the privilege of discovering, probing, and learning more and more about the character of God—for his glory and our joy.

May this book of meditations encourage your heart, strengthen your faith, and grow your affections for God. May you see more and more of the riches of the gospel of Jesus Christ, in whom "all the fullness of God was pleased to dwell" (Col. 1:19). And may you find yourself in a deeper, more-satisfying communion with your Savior and Lord.

❧ 2 ❧

God is God

SCRIPTURE MEDITATION

Be still and know that I am God. I will be exalted among the nations, I will be exalted in the earth!

Psalm 46:10

PRAYER

Heavenly Father, you are God and I am not. You are infinite and I am finite. You are powerful and I am weak. As I meditate upon your character, I pray that you would apply the truths of your Word to my life by your Spirit. Would you bring to my mind areas in my life that need change, encouragement, and peace? I desire to exalt you now as I meditate on the truth that you are not just the God of the universe—eternal and sovereign—but *my* God. As your sheep, I come to you, my Shepherd, in search of green pastures and still waters so that you might restore my soul. I pray this in Jesus' name. Amen.

*J*N BIBLICAL PERSPECTIVE

"In God we Trust" is printed on the back of every U.S. dollar bill. But *who* is the God we "trust?" And who are the "we" that trust that God? Many people believe that the God of the Christian faith is the same God as the god of the Islamic faith or the Hindu faith or of any number of other religions. But the God of Scripture—the true and living God—is vastly different.

One of the fundamental differences is that we believe in a God who eternally exists as three Persons, as God the *Trinity*: God the Father, God the Son, and God the Holy Spirit. These three Persons share the same essence and enjoy perfect unity forever (Heb. 1:3). None is greater than the other and none is inferior and they are not three gods. He is one God (Deut. 6:4), who exists in three persons forever (Matt. 28:19; 2 Cor. 13:14).

In Psalm 46:10, God exhorts his people: "Be still and know that I am God." The context is one of God bringing battle and war to an end. He then turns from the indicative—what he's done—to the imperative—what he requires of his people. "Be still," then can be viewed as a ceasing from battle. As you meditate on this verse, there are a few things to keep in mind.

First, this isn't simply a good suggestion; it's a *command*! In other words, this is a matter of obedience to God. But as much as it brings God glory, we partake of him in this delightful duty.

Second, God tells us to "be still." As mentioned, the context is one of battle. But how may this apply to you? Is there a sense in which you are "fighting" for reputation, significance, or any number of selfish endeavors? Indeed, stillness is a resting from sin and a resting in God in the midst of busy schedules. Between school, jobs, family, sports, and friends, being still seems very unfamiliar to many of us. The world is continually enticing us to fill our schedules and calendars with more and more. In addition, the idea of a Sabbath rest on the Lord's Day (Sunday) has virtually been lost in the dust of football, homework, or cleaning the house. We need to hear this message of stillness before a holy and gracious God.

Third, we are commanded to "know" something about God. The kind of knowing here isn't an empty knowledge, but a faith-filled, loving knowledge. In the New Testament, Paul prays for the Philippian church by saying, "It is my prayer that your love may abound more and more with knowledge and all discernment" (Phil. 1:9). Even the demons believe and know that God is God (Js. 2:19), but God calls us to a knowledge of him that draws our affections and faith together into a life that glorifies and exalts him.

Fourth, God tells us to know that he is *God*. Being the God of the Bible means that he is perfectly and completely sovereign, holy, wise, just, good, gracious, loving, and faithful (among many other characteristics). He commands us to *know* him. Jesus echoed this when he prayed, "And this is eternal life, that they know you the only true God, and Jesus Christ whom you have sent" (Jn. 17:3).

Finally, Psalm 46:10 tells us that God will be exalted among the nations and in the earth. This not only happened in its immediate Jewish context, but has continued to happen down through the ages and will find its final expression when we gather around the heavenly throne as people from "every nation, from all tribes and peoples and languages" (Rev. 7:9).

God the Father planned our redemption. God the Son accomplished our redemption. God the Holy Spirit applies our redemption. Though we deserve death as the payment of our sin (Rom. 6:23), God is gracious and has sent his only Son to be our substitute on the cross. Though we have been spared eternal separation from God, he did not spare his own Son, but gave him up for us all (Rom. 8:32).

*R*EFLECTION QUESTIONS

What are some initial thoughts that come to your mind when you think of the phrase, "God is God?"

This passage tells us to "be still." Do you find that your life is too busy? Do you find it difficult to spend time with God, to read his Word, or to pray? Are there activities that you could cut out for a season?

What are some things that you could do to increase your knowledge of and love for God? Are you willing to make these things a priority in your daily life? How?

How might the sin of pride hinder your recognition that God is God?

What do you think it means to "exalt" God at school, at work, or in your home?

How is it that God can say with full confidence, "I *will* be exalted?" What is at least one thing that says about his character?

*D*IGGING DEEPER

- That God is three Persons in one Godhead rightly points to the truth that he is *relational*. Genesis 1:27 says that we are created "in his image," which means (in part) that we are created for relationship—with God and with others. The unity of the community that we share with one another as the church should reflect the unity of the community of the Trinity.

- The development of Trinitarian theology took center stage over the first five centuries of the Christian church. The result of these labors can be found in confessions like the Nicene Creed completed at the First Council of Constantinople (381 A. D.) or the Chalcedonian Creed (451 A.D.).
- Many people today want to say that God is *only* loving or *only* gracious. But God is *perfectly* loving and *perfectly* gracious. He is also *perfectly* just and *perfectly* holy. We cannot limit God's attributes to a few things we think are nice. Rather, we must adjust our thinking and pattern our minds after God's Word.
- See also Gerald Bray, *The Doctrine of God* (Downers Grove: InterVarsity Press, 1993) and R. C. Sproul, *The Character of God: Discovering the God Who Is* (Ventua, California: Regal, 1995).

❖ 3 ❖

God is Sovereign

SCRIPTURE MEDITATION

Listen to me, O house of Jacob, all the remnant of the house of Israel, who have been borne by me from before your birth, carried from the womb, even to your old age I am he, and to gray hairs I will carry you. I have made, and I will bear; I will carry and will save. To whom will you liken me and make me equal, and compare me, that we may be alike? Remember this and stand firm, recall it to mind, you transgressors, remember the former things of old; for I am God, and there is no other; I am God, and there is none like me, declaring the end from the beginning, and from ancient times things not yet done, saying, 'My counsel shall stand, and I will accomplish all my purpose,' calling a bird of prey from the east, the man of my counsel from a far country. I have spoken, and I will bring it to pass; I have purposed, and I will do it.

Isaiah 46:3-5, 8-11

PRAYER

Heavenly Father, nothing is outside of your absolute control and power. I praise you that you uphold the universe by the word of your power and that nothing can thwart your plans. Now, as I enter into this meditation on your sovereignty, would you soften my heart and make me teachable to understand more of your character, so that I may have greater faith and delight in you and in your plans for my life. I pray this in the strong name of Jesus. Amen.

IN BIBLICAL PERSPECTIVE

That God is sovereign means that he is in absolute control over all things. Not the tiniest molecule, the fiercest tornado, or wisest thought is outside the control of God. He does what pleases him and nothing and no one can throw a wrench in his divine plan. From Adam's Fall in the Garden of Eden (Gen. 2) to the death of Christ on the cross (Acts 2:23) to the coming of Christ at the last judgment (1 Thess. 4:15-17), all actions and events that take place, happen under the sovereign hand of God.

Practically speaking, God's sovereignty is displayed in both his *eternal decrees* as well as day-to-day *providence*. His eternal decrees include his electing love, which has predestined—from before the foundation of the world—those who would believe in him (Eph. 1:4-6; Rom. 8:29). In other words, God has graciously chosen a people from before time began to be *his* people—loved and cherished (1 Thess. 1:4). These decrees also include all of his promises made throughout Scripture. If God were not in complete control, he could not promise anything and be able to follow through with those promises. In fact, we could not trust God at all because something else could thwart his promises. But there is nothing that is outside of God's governing power, wisdom, and control.

The other way that we see God's sovereignty displayed is in his providence. God's providence, as the *Westminster Shorter Catechism* explains, is "his most holy, wise, and powerful preserving and governing all his creatures, and all their actions." Proverbs 16:33 states: "The lot is cast into the lap, but its every decision is from the LORD." Providence refers to the expression and action of God's sovereignty. As light shines from the sun, so providence shines from God's sovereignty. They go hand-in-hand.

At first, the attribute of God's sovereignty might cause you to shrink in self-defense: "If God is really this powerful and have this much control, doesn't that just make me a robot, with no real choice or freedom?" But J. I. Packer writes, "That God's rational creatures, angelic and human, have free agency (power of personal decision as to what they shall do) is clear in Scripture throughout."[2] In other words, while God is absolutely sovereign over all things, we do have certain abilities and choices.

Unbelievers, to be clear, do not have free moral choice. Before receiving salvation in Christ, all of humanity is dead in sin (Eph. 2:1), unable to even long for God apart from his initiating grace (Jn. 3:3; 6:44; Rom. 8:7). But when God's grace breaks into the sinner's heart, he or she receives a new heart (Ezek. 36:26), one that responds with faith, love, and freedom. God is sovereign; man is responsible. Both hold together in a mysterious harmony. "Man plans his ways, but the LORD establishes his steps" (Prov. 16:9).

It is beyond the scope of this brief meditation to explore the relationship between God's sovereignty and human suffering, but suffice it to say that God is in control of all things, including human suffering. There are many reasons why God would allow suffering, from sharing in the sufferings of Christ (Phil. 3:10) to bringing glory to God (Jn. 21:19) to savoring *him* as the all-satisfying Savior that he is (Ps. 73:25-26) rather than the fleeting pleasures of this earthly life. In any case, it is important to remember that you and I are on an earthly pilgrimage to a heavenly home.

Even the death of God's own Son was part of "Plan A." When Peter preached at Pentecost in Acts 2, he boldly proclaimed that "this Jesus, delivered up according to the definite plan and foreknowledge of God, you crucified and killed by the hands of lawless men" (v. 23). The Old Testament prophet, Isaiah, looked ahead to the suffering Christ and wrote that "it was the will of the LORD to crush him" (Is. 53:10). The Son was crushed for you. The Son was forsaken on your behalf. The Son experienced hell so that you would never have to. Indeed, "with his stripes, we are healed" (Is. 53:5).

If Jesus Christ is your Savior and Lord, God promises his providential and loving care: "And we know that for those who love God all things work together for good, for those who are called according to his purpose" (Rom. 8:28). God's sovereignty should be a source of great comfort to your soul. You are held by a love unlike anything else in all of creation. You are held by a steadfast love that won't let you go (Rom. 8:39). Moreover, nothing will be able to snatch you out of the hands of your Savior (Jn. 10:28)!

REFLECTION QUESTIONS

In Isaiah 46:3-5, God communicates that from birth to "gray hairs" he will *carry* his people. What do you think he is trying to communicate to them? How might this affect your view of life?

In our passage, God talks of listening (v. 3), remembering (v. 8, 9), and recalling (v. 8). Take a few moments now and recall God's works in your life—how he has preserved you until now and graciously led you from birth. Why might thinking about these things be a difficult task?

What promise do you find in verse 4? "Even to your old age I am he, and to gray hairs I will carry you. I have made, and I will bear; I will carry and will save."

Verse 9 reads, "For I am God, and there is no other." Are there any "gods" or idols in your life right now that are hindering your worship of the true and living God? (Note: you might be worshipping what you are afraid of losing, including reputation, security, money, or people).

Verse 10 tells us that God declares "the end from the beginning and from ancient times things not yet done." How might this truth comfort your soul, in whatever circumstances you are in right now?

If God were not in complete control, could you trust him to keep any promise? Why or why not?

Just before his arrest, Jesus prayed about his impending suffering, "Not my will, but yours, be done" (Lk. 22:42). How might this inform how *we* ought to pray?

*D*IGGING DEEPER

- Other Scripture passages on God's sovereignty include Genesis 12:1-3; 50:20; Exodus 15:18; Psalm 33; 47; 93; 97; 115:3; Proverbs 16; Isaiah 24:23; Daniel 4:34; Matthew 10:29-31; Acts 13:26-39; Ephesians 1:10; and Revelation 1:4-8.

- Take some time and meditate on Philippians 2:12-13, where Paul exhorts the Philippians to "work out your own salvation with fear and trembling, for it is God who works in you, both to will and to work for his good pleasure." In this, man is responsible and given a charge. Yet, God remains sovereign as the One who works in us for his good pleasure.

- See also A. W. Pink, *The Sovereignty of God* (Edinburgh: Banner of Truth, 2009).

God is Holy

SCRIPTURE MEDITATION

And they sing the song of Moses, the servant of God, and the song of the Lamb, saying, Great and amazing are your deeds, O Lord God the Almighty! Just and true are your ways, O King of the nations! Who will not fear, O Lord, and glorify your name? For you alone are holy. All nations will come and worship you, for your righteous acts have been revealed.

Revelation 15:3-4

PRAYER

Heavenly Father, there is none like you. You alone are high and lifted up and worthy of my worship. Indeed, you are holy, holy, holy. As your child, I ask now that you would tune my heart towards yours and shape my mind by the power of your Word.

Would you be pleased with the meditation of my soul, I pray, in Jesus' name. Amen.

$\mathcal{I}$N BIBLICAL PERSPECTIVE

Can you think of a time when you have been the stranger? Or maybe you might be able to think of a time when you have felt completely different from other people? Similarly, God is altogether different from us. He is in complete control; we are not. He is perfect and righteous; we are not. He is God; we are not.

The holiness of God points to two specific elements of God's character. First, it points to the fact that God is fully set apart and different from anything and anybody else. Second, it points to the fact that he is morally righteous in his manifold perfections. In Genesis 2:3, God set apart the seventh day as "holy," which means it was to be *different* from all the other days. In Exodus 3:5, God tells Moses that the ground on which he stood was "holy" ground, which means that it was set apart and *different*. Paul tells Timothy that whoever is cleansed from sin is "set apart as holy" (2 Tim. 2:21). Being holy, in the first place, then, means that God is altogether different and set apart in glory, power, wisdom, righteousness, authority, goodness, love, truth, grace, and knowledge.

But holiness also refers to God's perfect righteous character. A. W. Pink writes, "The sum of all moral excellency is found in him."[3] No other purity comes close to the purity of God. He holds the full measure of all that is good and right. Every act, thought, and intent of God is completely righteous and perfect. He does not err, fail, nor does he act unjustly toward his creation. God's commandments, too, are holy. They are perfect, right, and true.

They are different from the law of man for they are derived from a holy and righteous God.

In Isaiah 6, the prophet records the seraphim calling out, "Holy, holy, holy is the LORD of hosts; the whole earth is full of his glory" (Is. 6:3). Likewise, the apostle John writes of the heavenly courts of praise: "Holy, holy, holy, is the Lord God Almighty, who was and is and is to come" (Rev. 4:8). The repetition is the superlative—as in high, higher, highest. That the biblical writers attest to the thrice-holy God is an explicit reference that there exists no one like God. He is altogether different and set apart, while manifesting the full sum of moral perfection.

Not only is God holy, but he calls us to holiness—perfect moral obedience (Lev. 11:44; 1 Pet. 1:15). Many people today think that God simply wants us to try our hardest. But that is not a biblical concept of the Christian life. God calls us to perfection and holiness. "But there's no way!" you might be saying. Ah, but there is a Way—*the* Way, the Truth and the Life (Jn. 14:6)!

While we are called to perfect holiness, we have fallen short of this glory of God (Rom. 3:23) and the wages of our sin is death (Rom. 6:23). Because God is holy, he must punish sin. Sin cannot stand for one second before a holy and righteous God. In fact, the most fundamental question of life is: "How can an unholy person stand in the presence of a holy God?"

But God, who is rich in mercy, sent his only Son into this world to become our substitute (Eph. 2:4). All of our filthiness, sin, blemishes, and *un*holiness was placed on Christ and he nailed it to the cross, thereby cancelling the record of debt that stood against us (Col. 2:14). In return, the perfect record of Jesus' obedience—his righteousness—was credited to our account. By faith, we are so unified with him that when God looks upon us, he sees the righteousness and the holy record of his own Son, Jesus Christ.

REFLECTION QUESTIONS

In Revelation 15, the apostle John imparts a vision of heavenly worship around the throne. The heartbeat of this worship is the "song of the Lamb." Why do you think the sacrificial lambs in the Old Testament (c.f. Leviticus) had to be "without blemish" to (temporarily) atone for the sins of God's people?

How do those Old Testament "unblemished lambs" point to *the* Lamb of God, Jesus Christ?

How does God being "just and true" (v. 3) relate to God being holy?

How does God's "righteous acts" (v. 4) relate to God being holy?

When you think of God being holy, what comes to your mind about yourself? Does the thought of God's holiness evoke any immediate response in your heart?

Throughout Paul's epistles, he calls various Christians, "saints," which in the Greek literally means *holy ones.* If we are not—in and of ourselves—holy, then how can Paul call imperfect, unholy, believers "holy?"

*D*IGGING DEEPER

- Other Scripture passages on the holiness of God include Exodus 15:11; Leviticus 11:44; 2 Chronicles 20:21; Isaiah 6:3; Psalm 30:4; 89:35; 110:3; 145:17; Mark 1:24; John 6:69; 1 Peter 1:15; 1 John 1:5; and Revelation 4:8.
- The sacraments are one example of something that is holy that we partake of in the Christian life. In fact, part of the word "sacred" is derived from an understanding of holiness.
- Another clear example of something set apart is the Bible, God's *holy* Word. God's Word is unlike any other book. It is fully inspired by the Holy Spirit and, therefore, comes ultimately from a divine author (2 Tim. 3:16; 2 Pet. 1:21).

Being "holy" would appropriately refer to it being wholly different, set apart, true, and right.

- See also R. C. Sproul, *The Holiness of God* (Carol Stream, Illinois: Tyndale House Publishers, 2000) and Stephen Charnock, *The Existence and Attributes of God* (Grand Rapids: Baker Books, 1996).

❊ 5 ❊

God is Faithful

SCRIPTURE MEDITATION

Now may the God of peace himself sanctify you completely, and may your whole spirit and soul and body be kept blameless at the coming of our Lord Jesus Christ. He who calls you is faithful; he will surely do it.

1 Thessalonians 5:23, 24

PRAYER

Heavenly Father, I praise you that you are perfectly committed to me, even when I am not committed to you. Thank you for your steadfast love and faithfulness to your children and that you will never let us go. You will never leave us nor forsake us. As I look now to this attribute of your faithfulness and meditate upon it, would you expose sins that I am harboring and bring me to a place of delight in your grace. Would you apply your holy Word to my life this day. I pray this in Christ's name. Amen.

$\mathcal{I}$N BIBLICAL PERSPECTIVE

Since the mid-1900s, America has witnessed a rapid breakdown of the family. Almost half of Americans polled today don't believe that marriage is even necessary. Many think that marriage is simply about "feeling" love, rather than commitment in a bound relationship for the glory of God. We are taught to be committed to something only so long as we are happy. It's all about our happiness and good feelings, rather than to reflect the covenant-keeping relationship between Christ and his bride (Eph. 5:25-32).

Church life is no different. As soon as we don't like the positioning of the tables, the smell of the flowers, the sound of the guitar, or the length of the sermon, we begin looking around for a church that will suit our tastes. In other words, commitment is thrown to the back seat and happiness drives the course of our relationships. The irony, of course, is that commitment shines brightest in times of sufferings, hardship, and difficulty. That's why wedding vows include being rich and poor, sickness and health, for better or worse. It's in the hard times that commitment is seen most clearly.

God understands commitment and faithfulness fully because it is part of his character. Throughout the Old Testament, Israel played the part of the prostitute—turning after "lovers" of this world rather than resting in the true Lover of her soul (Ezek. 16; Hos.). But God remained faithful to them. He was loyal, steadfast, committed, and bound to them—despite Israel's great unfaithfulness to him.

One of the clearest expressions of this is seen in the Hebrew word, *chesed*, which is translated into English as "loyal love," "steadfast love," "unfailing love," "committed love," or "covenant love." Consider these passages from the Psalter:

> *All the paths of the LORD are steadfast love and faithfulness* (Ps. 25:10).

> *For you, O Lord, are good and forgiving, abounding in steadfast love to all who call upon you* (Ps. 86:5).

> *Righteousness and justice are the foundation of your throne; steadfast love and faithfulness go before you* (Ps. 89:14).

> *Satisfy us in the morning with your steadfast love, that we may rejoice and be glad all our days* (Ps. 90:14).

> *For the LORD is good; his steadfast love endures forever, and his faithfulness to all generations* (Ps. 100:5).

> *For great is his steadfast love toward us, and the faithfulness of the LORD endures forever* (Psalm 117:2).

Notice the close relationship between God's steadfast love (*chesed*) and God's faithfulness. God's love doesn't fail. It doesn't ebb and flow with the tide of emotionalism. God's covenant promise is that he will remain our God and we will remain his people (Ex. 6:7; Jer. 30:22).

One of the greatest rewards of commitment and faithfulness is *intimacy.* Having an intimate relationship with somebody means knowing them—faults and all—and loving them anyway. It's the wonderful effect of a harmonious blend of knowledge and love. God seeks intimate fellowship with his people. He knows us completely and loves us *anyway* because we are "in Christ." The amazing thing about the gospel is that God gets glory when we find our satisfaction and joy in him. We experience intimacy with him when we know him and love him because he has first known and loved us (1 Jn. 4:19).

Your love for God follows your knowledge of God. Therefore, let the knowledge of God's faithfulness draw your affections toward him and you will find deep and satisfying intimacy with the Lover of your soul!

The more and more you rest in the faithfulness of God, the more faithfulness will be evidenced as a fruit of the Spirit in your own life (Gal. 5:22). The more you trust in God's faithfulness to forgive sin (1 Jn. 1:9), the more you will find strength to fight sin. The more you look unto God's faithfulness *in* your suffering, the more you will find peace, comfort, and joy. Consider Jeremiah's praise in the midst of suffering: "The steadfast love of the LORD never ceases; his mercies never come to an end; they are new every morning; great is your faithfulness" (Lam. 3:22, 23). God's faithfulness gives believers the right motivation and resource to begin a life of faithfulness to him.

REFLECTION QUESTIONS

Have you ever battled the same sin over and over? You might have even made a promise to God that you would "never do that again!" How might reflecting on God's faithfulness to you give you spiritual strength to resist sin in the future?

In 1 Thessalonians 5:23, God promises to "sanctify you completely." That means that, until you reach heaven, you will always need grace. The promise is sure, but the journey is ahead. Can you see real tangible signs of growth in your own Christian journey?

Our text says, "He who calls you is faithful." God never calls anybody without also giving them the resources to finish the race. What are some resources that God has given us to grow in our knowledge of and love for God?

How can the truth of God's faithful, steadfast love comfort your soul?

Do you have any truly intimate friendships with people who know the good, the bad, and the ugly about you and love you *anyway*? What might hinder you building such a relationship?

Jesus Christ was perfectly faithful in keeping all of God's commandments and laws—*on your behalf.* The credit and merit of his perfect obedience is transferred to you by simply believing him to be your Savior and Lord. How might this truth free you from pretending or performing that you are a "good" Christian all of the time?

$\mathcal{D}$IGGING DEEPER

- Other Scripture passages on God's faithfulness include Numbers 23:19; Deuteronomy 7:9; Psalm 36:5; 86:15; 100:5; 117:2; 145:13; Lamentations 3:22,23; Isaiah 11:5;

49:7; 1 Corinthians 1:9; 10:13; 2 Thessalonians 3:3; 2 Timothy 2:19; Hebrews 10:23; 1 Peter 4:19; 1 John 1:9; and Revelation 19:11.

- A lack of personal faithfulness is ultimately a lack of faith. If you had great faith in the greatness of the gospel, you would have greater faithfulness toward God. If you find that your faithfulness is more unfaithful than you would like, avail yourself to the means of God's transformative grace: God's Word, prayer, the sacraments, service, and grace-driven community.
- See also E. Calvin Beisner, *Psalms of Promise: Celebrating the Majesty and Faithfulness of God* (Phillipsburg: P&R Publishing, 1994).

❧ 6 ❧

God is Wise

Scripture Meditation

Oh, the depth of the riches and wisdom and knowledge of God! How unsearchable are his judgments and how inscrutable his ways! For who has known the mind of the Lord, or who has been his counselor? Or who has given a gift to him that he might be repaid? For from him and through him and to him are all things. To him be glory forever. Amen.

Romans 11:33-36

Prayer

Heavenly Father, how often I succumb to thinking, in subtle ways, that I know more than you. I think that I know what's best for me and others and that my view is right. Would you break me of this pride so that I may recognize you as infinitely wise, all knowing, and all powerful. You know what is good, true, and right and you

---

guide my steps. Would you give me the humility and strength to not lean upon my own understanding, but continually look unto you for wisdom and guidance. I pray this in the name of my wise King and Lord, Jesus Christ. Amen.

*I*N BIBLICAL PERSPECTIVE

Biblical wisdom is right knowledge displayed rightly. That God is wise means that he perfectly displays perfect knowledge in his Word, in creation, in providence, and in redemption. Wisdom combines knowledge with righteousness. It is *right* knowledge displayed *rightly*. It has a moral quality to it in that it is—in its essence—good, true, and noble.

Wisdom is different than mere knowledge. A person can be very knowledgeable about something, but lack wisdom. For example, you can know all there is to know about calculus or the biology of a frog, but that doesn't mean that you know how to use that knowledge in everyday life. Human wisdom, therefore, is right knowledge displayed rightly, under the fear of the Lord, for the love of God and love of neighbor.

Ascribing wisdom to God is essentially placing your trust in his knowledge, power, and goodness. When we say that God is perfectly wise, we are saying that—according to his infinite knowledge—he always acts with the best perspective and the best means to display his glory. We trust in his plan for our lives because he is all-knowing, all-powerful, and good. As Proverbs 3 states:

> *Trust in the LORD with all your heart, and do not*
> *lean on your own understanding. In all your ways*

acknowledge him, and he will make straight your
paths (Prov. 3:5, 6).

The wisdom literature of the Old Testament includes the books of Job, Psalms, Proverbs, Ecclesiastes, and Song of Solomon.[4] In each of these, two clearly defined ways of living are presented: the way of the wise and the way of the fool. The wise keep the fear of the Lord before them and acknowledge him in every aspect of life. The fool, on the other hand, shuns the character of God and seeks to live life independently of God (much like Adam and Eve did in the Garden).

Proverbs 9:10 states, "The fear of the LORD is the beginning of wisdom, and the knowledge of the Holy One is insight." Fearing God means having a reverence and awe before him—in view of his holiness, glory, power, and might. Pride vanishes from the heart when a healthy fear of God comes in. But fearing God is the *beginning* of wisdom. It's the starting point and foundation of wisdom. True wisdom, then, has a God-centered approach to living—in every area of life. From school to work, from family to friends, being wise must start with a right knowledge and fear of God.

The more we align our thoughts and hearts with the thoughts of God found in his Word, the more we will appropriate and display godly wisdom because wisdom comes from God. James writes, "If any of you lacks wisdom, let him ask God, who gives generously to all without reproach" (Js. 1:5). It is easy to get tunnel-vision, especially in the midst of suffering. But godly wisdom sees day-to-day struggles from a heavenly perspective and lifts hearts to trust in a God who is infinitely wise, powerful, and good.

In addition, Paul teaches that God's wisdom is "manifold" (Eph. 3:10). It is interesting that in the Greek version of the Old

Testament,[5] the word used to describe Joseph's coat of many colors (Gen. 37:3) is the same word used in Ephesians 3:10 to talk of God's "manifold" wisdom. In other words, God's wisdom is like a multi-colored tapestry, weaved together in a beautiful display of mystery, goodness, grace, and truth.

It should also be noted that godly wisdom and worldly wisdom are often-times opposites. Paul writes in 1 Corinthians 1:21, "For since, in the wisdom of God, the world did not know God through wisdom, it pleased God through the folly of what we preach to save those who believe." Worldly wisdom cannot "find" God. A person cannot save himself by worldly wisdom—it must come by grace alone. The gospel is *foolishness* in the eyes of the world. We die to live and give to gain. Jesus wore a crown of thorns, not gold.

Finally, the wisdom of God is fully displayed in the person of Jesus Christ (1 Cor. 1:24), whom God has made *our* wisdom. Paul explains: "God is the source of your life in Christ Jesus, whom God made our wisdom and our righteousness and sanctification and redemption" (1 Cor. 1:30). By faith in Christ, he becomes our wisdom so that we now have the ability and freedom to know God as Father and his Son Jesus as Savior and Lord.

*R*EFLECTION QUESTIONS

In Romans, Paul unpacks the gospel message and the glorious grace of God in a salvation that is received by faith alone in the finished work of Christ alone. Here in Romans 11:33-36, Paul's language explodes into a chorus of praise. Theology erupted into doxology. How might meditating on the wisdom of God set your heart to praise him?

What do you think Paul is communicating when he says that God's judgments are "unsearchable" in context of Romans 11:33-36?

Do you know anybody who you might consider "wise?" Why would you say that he or she is wise? How might that characteristic reflect God's wisdom?

Romans 11:36 says, "For from him and through him and to him are all things." How might this truth relate to the wisdom of God?

Moses prays in Psalm 90:12, "So teach us to number our days that we may get a heart of wisdom." How might studying God's Word teach us about seeing our lives from an eternal perspective, so that we might get a "heart of wisdom?"

Do you have any important decisions coming up? Do you need wisdom? Take some time and ask God to grant you wisdom in making the right decision.

*D*IGGING DEEPER

- Some other Scripture passages on the wisdom of God include 1 Kings 4:29; Psalm 111:10; Proverbs 1:7; 9:10; Daniel 2:20; 1 Corinthians 1:18-31; Ephesians 3:10; and James 1:5; 3:17.
- See also Warren W. Wiersbe, *Be Wise: Discern the Difference Between Man's Knowledge and God's Wisdom* (Colorado Springs: David Cook, 2010).

❋ 7 ❋

God is Creator

SCRIPTURE MEDITATION

Who has measured the waters in the hollow of his hand and marked off the heavens with a span, enclosed the dust of the earth in a measure and weighed the mountains in scales and the hills in a balance? It is he who sits above the circle of the earth, and its inhabitants are like grasshoppers; who stretches out the heavens like a curtain, and spreads them like a tent to dwell in. Lift up your eyes on high and see: who created these? He who brings out their host by number, calling them all by name, by the greatness of his might and because he is strong in power not one is missing. Have you not known? Have you not heard? The LORD is the everlasting God, the Creator of the ends of the earth.

Isaiah 40:12, 22, 26, 28

$\mathcal{P}$RAYER

Heavenly Father, you have created me and I am fearfully and wonderfully made. You are my Creator and I am your creation. Would you now draw me close to you, to rest in your promises, and to enjoy fellowship with you. And would you give me a grateful heart that you alone are the Creator of the ends of the earth. I pray this in Jesus' name. Amen.

$\mathcal{I}$N BIBLICAL PERSPECTIVE

"In the beginning God, created the heavens and the earth" (Gen. 1:1). God created all things out of nothing by his word. God is the only non-created being from all eternity. The opening chapters of Genesis describe some of the details surrounding his creative power and the nature of the creation itself. "And God saw everything that he had made, and behold, it was very good" (Gen. 1:31). There is nothing intrinsically evil about God's creation as he created it.

The pinnacle of God's creation was the creation of man, whom he created in his own image—male and female (Gen. 1:27). Being created in the image of God means, first, that man was created to reflect God's communicable attributes, such as love, justice, mercy, kindness, goodness, and so forth. But being created in the image of God also means that *man was created for relationship*. As we saw in chapter 2, God exists as one God in three persons: the Father, the Son, and the Holy Spirit. Therefore, God is, in his essence, relational and has created us to have relationship with him and with others.

That God is Creator means that his creation serves as an echo and display of his handiwork, power, and wisdom. Creation is God's general revelation to his creatures, which attests to his eternal power and divine nature (Rom. 1:20). King David exclaims, "The heavens declare the glory of God, and the sky above proclaims his handiwork" (Ps. 19:1). This characteristic of God as Creator should serve to bring great humility to our souls as we consider his works. David, again, writes:

> When I look at your heavens, the work of your fingers, the moon and the stars, which you have set in place, what is man that you are mindful of him, and the son of man that you care for him (Ps. 8:3-4)?

We are to give praise to God, for we are fearfully and wonderfully made (Ps. 139:14). Before you were born, God knew all about you (cf. Jer. 1:5) and then you were "intricately woven" in your mother's womb (Ps. 139:15). God creates all things for his glory, including the birds of the air and the fish of the sea. And he has created *you* for his glory as well and rejoices over you with gladness (Zeph. 3:17).

It is also important to note that all three Persons of the Trinity were involved in creation. As the Spirit hovered over the face of the waters at creation (Gen. 1:2), so also Christ became the agent through whom God created the world. The apostle John writes, "All things were made through [Christ], and without him was not any thing made that was made" (Jn. 1:3). Likewise, Paul writes, "By [Christ] all things were created, in heaven and on earth, visible and invisible...all things were created through him and for him" (Col. 1:16). The writer of Hebrews also attests to involvement of

Jesus in creation, "through whom also he created the world" (Heb. 1:2).

But man is sin-filled and his heart is an idol factory,[6] bent on turning anything and everything into idols of worship. Paul explains in Romans that humanity has "exchanged the glory of the immortal God for images resembling mortal man and birds and animals and reptiles" (Rom. 1:23). As sinful men and women, we have turned to worship the creation instead of the Creator.

But God has sent his only eternal Son, to reconcile God's creation to himself. God's purpose in Christ is "to unite all things in him, things in heaven and things on earth" (Eph. 1:10). Paul writes, "In Christ God was reconciling the world to himself, not counting their trespasses against them" (2 Cor. 5:19), that "the creation itself will be set free from it bondage to decay and obtain the freedom of the glory of the children of God" (Rom. 8:21).

Therefore, "if anyone is in Christ, he is a new creation. The old has passed away; behold, the new has come" (2 Cor. 5:17). As God's new creation by faith in Jesus, we have been called to holiness by grace. Because we are saved by God's grace alone, he re-creates us as his "workmanship, created in Christ Jesus for good words, which God prepared beforehand, that we should walk in them" (Eph. 2:10). You are God's *workmanship* and his treasured masterpiece. God knows all about you because you are his creation.

From beginning to end, God is declared to be the eternal and wise God, the Creator of the ends of the earth. Not only does he create all things in the universe, "he upholds the universe by the word of his power" (Heb. 1:3). It is God who creates, who sustains, and who preserves his people for his glory. By faith in the eternal, *un*created Son—Jesus Christ—believers are made his new creation to the praise of his glory!

REFLECTION QUESTIONS

What do you think Isaiah is trying to communicate by his rhetorical question in Isaiah 40:12: "Who has measured the waters in the hollow of his hand and marked off the heavens with a span, enclosed the dust of the earth in a measure and weighed the mountains in scales and the hills in a balance?"

What other attributes of God comes to your mind when you read Isaiah 40:22: "It is he who sits above the circle of the earth, and its inhabitants are like grasshoppers; who stretches out the heavens like a curtain, and spreads them like a tent to dwell in?" Why?

Isaiah 40:26 tells us that not one star is missing in God's perfect creation. How might that relate to the nature of God's creative work?

Take a few minutes to reflect on Isaiah 40:28: "The LORD is the everlasting God, the Creator of the ends of the earth." What are some thoughts that come to your mind?

*D*IGGING DEEPER

- Some other Scripture passages on God as Creator include Genesis 1, 2; Psalm 8; 19:1-6; 139:13-16; 148:5; Ecclesiastes 12:1; Isaiah 42:5; Acts 17:26; Romans 8:19; 2 Corinthians 5:17; Ephesians 2:10, 15; Colossians 1:15-16; 1 Timothy 4:4; Hebrews 1:2; 1 Peter 4:19; and Revelation 10:6.
- God creates both instantly and through secondary means. Instantaneous creation would include salvation. An example of secondary creation would be the growth of a plant. For example, if you plant a seed in good soil and water it, the seed will sprout and grow. You can make a table, but again, the table comes from wood, which comes from a tree, which is from the seed, which God created. God as Creator, then, also means that he is the *source* of all things.
- See also Mark David Futato, *Creation: A Witness to the Wonder of God* (Phillipsburg: P&R Publishing, 2000).

❊ 8 ❊

God is Sustainer

SCRIPTURE MEDITATION

Cast your burden on the LORD, and he will sustain you; He will never permit the righteous to be moved.

Psalm 55:22

PRAYER

Heavenly Father, even now as I pray to you, you are sustaining my life—giving me breath and a beating heart. Thank you for sustaining my faith and preserving my life by your grace. I know that I am safe under your watchful care and that you are my great Shepherd. Would you make me lie down in the green pastures of your grace as I meditate on you as my Sustainer. I pray this in Jesus' name. Amen.

IN BIBLICAL PERSPECTIVE

To sustain means to uphold, to keep, or to preserve. It means not giving up. God not only creates everything, but *sustains* everything. From the air you are breathing right now to your beating heart, God is keeping you alive for his glory.

God sustains us bodily here on earth until he calls us home to be with him in heaven. God sustains us spiritually, not letting anyone or anything snatch you out of Christ's sovereign hand (Jn. 10:28). God sustains us emotionally when we just can't bear the pain any longer. God sustains his whole creation, upholding the universe by the word of his power (Heb. 1:3). In all these ways and more, God is providentially and powerfully working to uphold you, keep you, and preserve you so that you will find joy, hope, and respond with a thankful heart.

The apostle Paul writes of the sustaining power of Christ in 1 Corinthians 1:4-9:

> *I give thanks to my God always for you because of the grace of God that was given you in Christ Jesus, that in every way you were enriched in him in all speech and all knowledge—even as the testimony about Christ was confirmed among you—so that you are not lacking in any spiritual gift, as you wait for the revealing of our Lord Jesus Christ, who will sustain you to the end, guiltless in the day of our Lord Jesus Christ. God is faithful, by whom you were called in to fellowship of his Son, Jesus Christ our Lord.*

What is amazing about this passage is that Paul links the faithfulness of God to the sustaining power of Christ. God as Sustainer is one aspect of him being faithful. God sustains our faith, even when we sometimes feel like casting it aside. One way he does this is by continually drawing us into fellowship with Jesus.

Enjoying communion and fellowship with Christ is a means by which God sustains his people. The basis of our communion with Christ is our union with Christ through faith in his saving work. We enter into fellowship through the application of God's Word, through prayer, through the sacraments, through service, and through grace-centered community.

One of the other great truths of Scripture is that, if you are a true believer in Christ, you can never lose your salvation. "And I am sure of this, that he who began a good work in you will bring it to completion at the day of Jesus Christ" (Phil. 1:6). While your fellowship with Christ may wax and wane, you will never lose your salvation. However, test your heart to see if you possess true faith. Even mustard-seed faith opens wide the gates of heaven and secures your eternal reward.

Meditate on these words of promise:

> *For I, the LORD your God, hold your right hand;*
> *it is I who say to you, 'Fear not, I am the one who*
> *helps you.'* (Is. 41:13).

> *God, the Lord, is my strength; he makes my feet like*
> *the deer's; he makes me tread on my high places*
> (Hab. 3:19).

My grace is sufficient for you, for my power is made perfect in weakness (2 Cor. 12:9).

He gives power to the faint, and to him who has no might he increases strength (Is. 40:29).

That God is Sustainer also dispels fear. A few verses earlier, God says, "Fear not, for I am with you" (Is. 41:10). The more that you rest in the power of God to sustain your life and faith, the more you will be able to fight the fear of man, the fear of death, and the fear of evil.

I mentioned that one of the ways that God sustains us is by his Word. The Bible's message is about Christ crucified and his victory over sin and death for us. God promises believers that "there is therefore now no condemnation for those who are in Christ Jesus" (Rom. 8:1). In other words, God's promises—found in his Word—sustain us. As the Psalmist prays: "Uphold me according to your promise, that I may live" (Ps. 119:116). Rest in the promises of God to sustain your faith, revive your soul, and bring delight to your heart.

*R*EFLECTION QUESTIONS

If God is your Sustainer, it should fill you with great hope. But why *hope*?

Psalm 55:22 tells us to cast our burden on the LORD. Do you have any burdens that you need to relinquish and cast before the Lord? List some things that you are struggling with at the moment and then meditate on Matthew 11:28-30.

How might casting a burden upon the Lord sustain you?

If you knew that you were completely safe and secure in Jesus—that you were fully accepted and loved—how might that affect your relationships with people around you?

What are some ways that God is sustaining you this very moment—physically, spiritually, or emotionally?

DIGGING DEEPER

- Some other Scripture passages on God as Sustainer include Deuteronomy 7:9; Isaiah 40:29-31; John 10:28; 1 Corinthians 1:4-9; Ephesians 1:14; Philippians 1:6; 2 Timothy 1:8-12; Hebrews 1:1-3; and Revelation 19:11.

- That God *sustains* implies something against which he would need to sustain us. There would be nothing special about sustaining us if there was no *need* to sustain us. In other words, what are we sustained *from*? There is a need for God's sustaining power. We are sinful and cannot sustain ourselves against the attacks of sin, the miseries of this life, and death itself. Can you think of any other reason that we *need* to be sustained?

- See also Burk Parsons, ed., *Assured by God: Living in the Fullness of God's Grace* (Phillipsburg: P&R Publishing, 2006).

❋ 9 ❋

God is Love

SCRIPTURE MEDITATION

So we have come to know and to believe the love that God has for us. God is love, and whoever abides in love abides in God, and God abides in him.

1 John 4:16

PRAYER

Heavenly Father, as I begin this meditation on your love, would you gently remind me of your great love for me. Would you remind me that you have so loved the world, that you gave your only Son, Jesus Christ. Would you give me a fresh perspective on your love and help me to be amazed at how faithful it is, how true it is, and how enduring it is. I pray this in the strong name of Jesus, my loving Lord. Amen.

*I*N BIBLICAL PERSPECTIVE

Love isn't just an attribute of God; it's his very nature. From all eternity the Father, Son, and Holy Spirit are held in a perfect unity of love. In fact, this is one of the reasons Jesus says in his prayer before his arrest that the Father "loved me before the foundation of the world" (Jn. 17:24). Paul writes that we, as God's elect, are blessed in Christ Jesus, "the Beloved" (Eph. 1:6).

We may appropriately call God, "the God of love." As you meditate on the God of love, rest in his Word: "May the Lord direct your hearts to the love of God and to the steadfastness of Christ" (2 Thess. 3:5). Stop and pray that this may be true of your own heart this day.

There are several amazing truths surrounding our passage for today in the fourth chapter of 1 John. First, John teaches us that Love is from God (v. 7). Any streams of love we exhibit come from the deep and wide river of love. Second, John points to the greatest expression of love:

> *In this the love of God was made manifest among us, that God sent his only Son into the world, so that we might live through him (v. 9).*

This, of course, echoes Romans 5:8, where Paul explains, "But God shows his love for us in that while we were still sinners, Christ died for us." The incarnation—God taking on flesh in the person of Jesus Christ—the life, death, and work of Christ is the greatest witness and display of divine love.

A third contextual truth surrounding our passage is that God's love is "perfected in us" (v. 12). The word in Greek for "perfected" here is the same word used by Jesus on the cross when he proclaimed, "It is finished" (Jn. 19:30)! Not only was our debt *paid in full*, but God's love for us was also *paid in full*. There can be nothing added or taken away from God's love for us. In other words, there is no more love to be "used up." His love is also unconditional; it cannot waver or fail. Because God's character is unchanging and because his love is based on his unchanging character, *his love is unchanging.*

Fourthly, John teaches, "There is no fear in love, but perfect love casts out fear" (v. 18). Perfect love isn't referring to *our* love, but to *God's* love. He is the only One with perfect love and he cast out our fear of others, of death, and of sin. If you know deep down that you are unconditionally loved by the King of the universe, what is there to fear? Death has been swallowed up in victory (1 Cor. 15:54)!

Fifthly, "we love because he first loved us" (v. 19). The only way men and women, boys and girls, can ever love God is only if God first gives them new hearts to love him (Ezek. 36:26). Our love is our response to his gracious love in the first place.

The final contextual truth surrounding our text for today is that we "ought to love one another" (v. 11). Our love should reflect the love of God. When asked about the greatest commandment, Jesus responded, "You shall love the Lord your God with all your heart and with all your soul and with all your mind" (Matt. 22:37). But he followed this answer with the *second* greatest commandment, "You shall love your neighbor as yourself" (v. 39). If we have been so loved by God, saved through the work of Christ, and sealed by the Holy Spirit (Eph. 1:13), then we should abound in our love for one another (1 Thess. 3:12).

ℛEFLECTION QUESTIONS

As you reflect on our passage in 1 John 4:16, do you see any difference between believing *in* the love of God and simply believing the love of God?

How would you define love? Would your definition match with the biblical perspective given in this chapter?

John teaches that "God is love." Can love be love if it is not expressed or given to another?

Simply take a few moments and abide in God's love. Rest in the knowledge that he loves *you* unconditionally, even right after you sin against him. Let your affections be stirred by God's amazing love for you.

What are some practical ways that you can "abide in God's love" on a regular basis?

How can the truth that "God is love" give you strength to love one another?

$\mathcal{D}$IGGING DEEPER

- Scripture passages on the love of God include Exodus 34:6; 2 Chronicles 5:13; Psalm 100:5; Jeremiah 31:3; John 3:16-17; 15:13; Romans 5:8; 8:35-39; 1 Corinthians 13; 2 Corinthians 5:14; Galatians 5:22; Ephesians 2:4; 5:2-25; Philippians 1:9; Colossians 3:14; 2 Thessalonians 2:16; 1 John 4; and Revelation 1:5.
- Discipline and love actually go together for the believer. Consider Hebrews 12:6, "For the Lord disciplines the one he loves." Believer, do not think your suffering is from wrath, but from love.
- Paul explains that we are to grow in our love *with knowledge.* "And this is my prayer that your love may abound more and more, with knowledge and all discernment" (Phil. 1:9). Jonathan Edwards once noted that our worship should have heat in the heart and light in the mind, but

no more heat than justified by light. What do you think he is communicating by saying that?

- See also John Piper, *Think: The Life of the Mind and the Love of God* (Wheaton: Crossway, 2010) and David Powlison, *God's Love: Better Than Unconditional* (Phillipsburg: P&R Publishing, 2001).

10

God is Gracious

Scripture Meditation

I will make all my goodness pass before you and proclaim before you my name 'The Lord.' And I will be gracious to whom I will be gracious, and will show mercy on whom I will show mercy.

Exodus 33:19

Prayer

Heavenly Father, I don't deserve life or salvation. I don't deserve *anything*, but death and hell forever. But you are gracious and merciful. It is by your grace alone that I am saved and can enjoy fellowship with you and with other believers in Christ. May your grace amaze me now as I peer into this attribute of your perfect character. Would your Spirit expand the elasticity of my soul to take in more and more of you and to rest in your grace this day. I pray in Jesus' name. Amen.

$\mathcal{I}$N BIBLICAL PERSPECTIVE

Many people today believe in a sense of entitlement. They might say things like, "I am entitled to this car or that house." "I deserve a higher-paying job or straight A's." If you listen to the radio or watch television for any length of time, advertisements are geared toward making you believe that you are entitled to whatever product they are trying to sell. They are led to believe that it is right—"just" even—for them to simply have whatever they want as if they *deserve* it.

But the biblical message gives an entirely different picture. When it speaks of what we deserve, the payment is vastly different. Consider the nature of our sinful hearts:

> *The LORD saw that the wickedness of man was great in the earth, and that every intention of the thoughts of his heart was only evil continually* (Gen. 6:5).

> *There is no one who does good, not even one* (Ps. 14:3).

> *The heart is deceitful above all things* (Jer. 17:9).

> *And you were dead in the trespasses and sins* (Eph. 2:1).

> *For all have sinned and fall short of the glory of God* (Rom. 3:23).

> *For the wages of sin is death* (Rom. 6:23).

It is clear from Scripture that all are sinful, lost, and without hope except in the sovereign grace of God. All deserve his divine wrath and judgment. In other words, it would be *fair* if everyone went to hell. But God is gracious and gives us what we don't deserve.

There is a subtle difference between grace and mercy. To be sure, God is both gracious and merciful. But the biblical view of grace is narrow and reserved only for his chosen people, the elect. A. W. Pink explains, "Grace is a perfection of the divine character which is exercised only toward the elect." He goes on to say, "Neither in the Old Testament nor in the New is the grace of God ever mentioned in connection with mankind generally."[7]

Mercy, on the other hand, "is over all that he has made" (Ps. 145:9). Mercy is not getting what you deserve or at least a temporary relief from what you deserve. It is only by his mercy that all of mankind isn't consumed immediately by divine wrath and justice. Believers, then, receive *both* grace and mercy.

The grace of God is his sovereign unmerited favor upon his sheep, the church, which is bride of Christ. Because grace is an attribute of God's character, it is eternal—even before it was actually extended to his people. Paul explains that God saved us, "not because of our works but because of his own purpose and grace, which he gave us in Christ Jesus before the ages began" (2 Tim. 1:9).

God's grace is also sovereign, given only to those whom he chooses. As God says in our passage for today, "I will be gracious to whom I will be gracious, and will show mercy on whom I will show mercy" (Ex. 33:19). God is completely sovereign to bestow divine favor on whomever he chooses.

God's grace is also a gift, which means that it is received freely apart from any payment of our own. Paul writes, "For by grace you have been saved through faith. And this is not your own doing;

it is the gift of God" (Eph. 2:8). Though the gift of grace costs you nothing, it cost Jesus his life. Jesus took your wages of sin upon himself so that you would receive the wages of righteousness and the gift of eternal life.

One of the purposes of God's law[8] was to show how sinful we truly are, which only highlights the wonder of grace all the more: "Now the law came in to increase the trespass, but where sin increased, grace abounded all the more" (Rom. 5:20).

Finally, we are to "grow in the grace and knowledge of our Lord and Savior Jesus Christ" (2 Pet. 3:18). Although we are counted completely forgiven and righteous through faith in Jesus, God continues to transform us daily until we reach the "fullness of Christ" (Eph. 4:13). It is by grace alone that we are saved. It is by grace alone that we find joy and hope in the gospel of Christ. It is by grace alone that "we live and move and have our being" (Acts 17:28). It is be grace alone that God pardons our sin and accepts us as righteous in his sight. And it is by grace alone that he will usher us one day into glory.

*R*EFLECTION QUESTIONS

Are there things that you believe you "deserve" or are entitled to? Think honestly about this question.

In our Scripture passage for today, why do you think God's name, "The Lord," is important as we consider God's grace? What about that title reveals more of the nature of God's grace?

Right now, can you think of how God is showing you *mercy* specifically? What is he withholding that you really deserve?

Take a few moments and consider the depths of your sin. Do you see it for what it is, as cosmic treason against your Creator and Sustainer? Consider God's grace in saving you from your sin—placing that sin upon his only Son, who died in your place. What should your response be to such grace?

Do you ever think that you deserve God's blessing and favor more than another person? Are there people that you think that simply don't deserve any grace at all? Do you think that you deserve that grace?

How can you practically extend grace to people at work, school, or family members—especially when they have hurt you?

How does the gospel of grace give you the *right motivation* to serve God and others?

DIGGING DEEPER

- Other Scripture passages on the God of grace include Psalm 86:15; 103:8; 116:5; Amos 5:15; John 1:14; Acts 15:11; Romans 3:24; 5:20; 1 Corinthians 15:10; 2 Corinthians 8:9; 12:9; Ephesians 1:6; 2:8; Titus 2:11; 1 Peter 1:13; 5:10; and 2 Peter 3:18.
- If we think that grace is "deserved" it is no longer grace we are talking about. Grace is never deserved, but given freely by God who is sovereign.
- See also Sinclair Ferguson, *By Grace Alone: How the Grace of God Amazes Me* (Lake Mary, Florida: Reformation Trust Publishing, 2010); Jerry Bridges, *The Discipline of Grace: God's Role and Our Role in the Pursuit of Holiness* (Colorado Springs: NavPress, 2006); and Charles Spurgeon, *Grace: God's Unmerited Favor* (New Kensington, Pennsylvania: Whitaker House, 1996).

11

God is Just

SCRIPTURE MEDITATION

For I will proclaim the name of the LORD; ascribe greatness to our God! The Rock, his work is perfect, for all his ways are justice. A God of faithfulness and without iniquity, just and upright is he.

Deuteronomy 32:3, 4

PRAYER

Heavenly Father, as I quiet my mind and heart now to consider and ponder your justice, would you remind me of the payment for my sin in the death of Christ—that he bore your wrath to satisfy your justice in punishing sin, *my* sin. I am grateful that you are a just God, calling me to do justice, to love kindness, and to walk humbly with you. Would you teach me more of your just character so that I would understand more about your perfect grace, displayed in the gospel of your Son, Jesus. I pray this in his name. Amen.

JN BIBLICAL PERSPECTIVE

That God is *just* can be understood in two related ways. First, justice is a virtue of God in that he is an equitable ruler of all. The moral bar of this attribute is his righteousness. God is just in that he has perfect integrity of moral character and righteous virtue. Sin, therefore, cannot be tolerated or go unpunished under his sovereign rule. Consider Romans 1:32: "Though they know God's decree that those who practice such things deserve to die, they not only do them but give approval to those who practice them."

The second way that we understand God's justice is in how he *expresses* his just character—as either reward or punishment. As the Psalmist declares, "The King in his might loves justice. You have established equity; you have executed justice and righteousness in Jacob" (Ps. 99:4). Or consider Paul's teaching in Romans 2:6, "He will render to each one according to his works."

In view of God who rewards the obedient, the reward is not based on strict merit, but according to his promises of his grace and agreement. That is why Isaiah calls our righteousness, "a polluted garment" (Is. 64:6). He is a Rewarder because he is a God who is faithful to his own promises and clothes us with *his* righteousness by faith (cf. Gen. 15:6; Phil. 3:9).

In view of God who punishes sin, his justice is an expression of divine wrath. This characteristic is seen in places like 2 Thessalonians 1:8, where it understands Jesus "inflicting vengeance on those who do not know God and on those who do not obey the gospel of our Lord Jesus." Louis Berkhof explains, "The primary purpose of the punishment of sin is the maintenance of right and justice."[9]

The justice of God should evoke a sense of fear and dread for the lost and a sense of gratitude for the saved. As believers, we can take comfort that "God has not destined us for wrath, but to obtain salvation through our Lord Jesus Christ" (1 Thess. 5:9).

So how is a person counted "right" before God? You are counted righteous and "not guilty" before God by *believing* that Jesus lived a perfect life for you and died to pay the penalty for your sins. This transaction between the Christian and Christ "was to show [God's] righteousness...so that he might be just and the justifier of the one who has faith in Jesus" (Rom. 3:26).

Righteousness is the earned merit of perfect obedience to God. We are not perfect nor obedient so we are not righteous. But Jesus perfectly obeyed all of the law of God *for us* who believe. That perfect record, then, is transferred to your account and God declares you to be "righteous" because you are united to his righteous Son. Paul writes, "For our sake he made him to be sin who knew no sin, so that in him we might become the righteousness of God" (2 Cor. 5:21). This transaction was both an expression of divine love and grace as well as an effectual means by which he satisfied his divine justice.

A final word needs to be said about God's justice as a restoration of the broken, the outcast, the poor, the orphan, and the widow. God is in the business of looking after the outcast and the broken—keeping them central in the ministry of his people. Some have called this "social justice" while others call it "mercy ministry." Either way, God's Word is full of exhortations and commands to seek justice for the oppressed. Consider a few of them:

He executes justice for the fatherless and the widow, and love the sojourner, giving him food and clothing (Deut. 10:18).

Learn to do good; seek justice, correct oppression; bring justice to the fatherless, plead the widow's cause (Is. 1:17).

What does the LORD require of you but to do justice, and to love kindness, and to walk humbly with your God (Mic. 6:8).

Woe to you, scribes and Pharisees, hypocrites! For you tithe mint and dill and cumin, and have neglected the weightier matters of the law: justice and mercy and faithfulness (Matt. 23:23).

Religion that is pure and undefiled before God, the Father is this: to visit orphans and widows in their affliction, and to keep oneself unstained from the world (Js. 1:27).

God's justice, then, is part of God's character. It is an expression of reward for righteousness and punishment for sin, and it is a desire to see equity among his people. May your meditation on the justice of God translate into a gospel-driven action for expressing his justice in the broken world around you.

REFLECTION QUESTIONS

As a just God, why does he require punishment for sin?

What part does justice play in the reconciliation of your relationship with God? What part does Jesus play in that reconciliation?

Why did Jesus have to be perfect and righteous to be our substitute on the cross?

Our passage in Deuteronomy 32 states that God is both faithful and just. How do these two attributes relate? What if God was just only *some* of the time? Why does he have to be both at the same time?

We were created in God's image (Gen. 1:27), which means, in part, that we are to reflect his character. How can you practically reflect God's justice in the world, especially to the poor, the outcast, the widow, and the orphan?

*D*IGGING DEEPER

- Other Scripture passages on the justice of God include Deuteronomy 7:9-13; 2 Chronicles 6:15; Psalm 99:4; Isaiah 1:17; 3:10, 11; Micah 6:8; 7:20; Matthew 25:41; Luke 17:10; Romans 1:32; 2:6; 6:23; 1 Corinthians 4:7; 2 Thessalonians 1:8; James 1:27; and 1 Peter 1:17.
- "Doing justice" for the outcast, the poor, and the broken is a matter of obedience, not just sympathy.
- Being a "just society" is one that not only has laws, but enforces those laws. It also means that those laws apply to all and that there is no discrimination.
- See also Timothy Keller, *Generous Justice: How God's Grace Makes Us Just* (New York: Dutton, 2010) and J. I. Packer, *Knowing God* (Downers Grove: IVP Books, 1993).

12

God is Glorious

SCRIPTURE MEDITATION

For God, who said, "Let light shine out of darkness," has shone in our hearts to give the light of the knowledge of the glory of God in the face of Jesus Christ. But we have this treasure in jars of clay, to show that the surpassing power belongs to God and not to us.

2 Corinthians 4:6, 7

PRAYER

Heavenly Father, you are of supreme value and worth. You are glorious in your manifold character. You are the greatest Treasure in the universe and, by your grace, you have become *my* Treasure. I am but a clay pot, broken and weak. And yet, you have placed within me the glories of your gospel. As I meditate upon your glory, would you fill me with awe and wonder and bring me unto your throne of grace. I pray this in Christ's name. Amen.

$\mathcal{I}$N BIBLICAL PERSPECTIVE

God's glory refers specifically to his divine essence and ultimate greatness. It is the display of the sum total of God's manifold perfections. As the sun shines beams of light, so God's character shines beams of glory. The apostle John explains,

> *And I saw no temple in the city, for its temple is the Lord God the Almighty and the Lamb. And the city has no need of sun or moon to shine on it, for the glory of God gives it light, and its lamp is the Lamb* (Rev. 21:22-23).

God's glory, then, is the expression of his essential nature, which is also represented by his honor and his name.

Throughout the Bible, God repeatedly refers to his sovereign works, his revelation, and his covenant promises in relation to his *name*. Consider a few of these passages as they relate his glory to his name:

> *Ascribe to the LORD the glory due his name; worship the LORD in the splendor of holiness* (Ps. 29:2).

> *Shout for joy to God, all the earth; sing the glory of his name; give to him glorious praise* (Ps. 66:1, 2).

> *Help us, O God of our salvation, for the glory of your name* (Ps. 79:9).

His name is like directional marker—pointing to his character, promises, and mighty works. In other words, when we say that we "praise his name," we are saying that we praise his glorious attributes as they exist in his nature and as they are expressed throughout his creation.

In fact, creation itself bears witness to the glory of God: "The heavens declare the glory of God, and the sky above proclaims his handiwork" (Ps. 19:1). As Isaiah is taken aback by his vision of the Lord, he tells of the proclamation of the seraphim: "Holy, holy, holy is the LORD of hosts; the whole earth is full of his glory" (Is. 6:3). Creation, then, also points—like a directional arrow—to God's perfect character and attributes.

Similarly, the Bible speaks of "giving glory" to God or "glorifying" him: "Let them give glory to the LORD and declare his praise" (Is. 42:12). In this sense, giving glory to God means praising him for his worth, his character, and simply for who he is. In fact, everything we do, we should seek to give him glory (praise). As Paul writes, "So, whether you eat or drink, or whatever you do, do all to the glory of God" (1 Cor. 10:31). When we "give" glory to God, we are not literally giving him something as if he lacked a part of holiness or essential greatness. Rather, we are acknowledging and ascribing praise *because* of his greatness and perfect character. Glory and praise, as our response to the expression of his character, are synonymous (Phil. 1:11). When we "glorify" his name (cf. Ps. 86:9; Lk. 2:20), we are praising him and lifting him up as the only true and living God.

The *greatest* expression, however, of God's glory is in the incarnation (God becoming man) of his eternal Son, Jesus Christ. In Jesus, we find the full display of God's manifold character. Jesus has taken sinners, who have fallen short of the glory of God (Rom. 3:23), and has become their "hope of glory" (Col. 1:27). In other words, Jesus—in whom "all the fullness of God was pleased to dwell (Col. 1:19)—has set up residence in our hearts by his Spirit (Gal. 4:6). He now grants us access to not only come directly before God's throne of grace (Heb. 4:16), but also to enter glory itself—our heavenly home (Col. 3:4).

The apostle Paul writes, "And we all, with unveiled face, beholding the glory of the Lord, are being transformed into the same image from one degree of glory to another" (2 Cor. 3:18). Likewise, he explains, Jesus himself "will transform our lowly body to be like his glorious body" (Phil. 3:21). As pilgrims, we make our way through this troubled life, looking unto the founder and perfecter of our faith (Heb. 12:2), until we are *glorified* in the presence of the glory of God (Rom. 8:30).

*R*EFLECTION QUESTIONS

What do you think "darkness" refers to in 2 Corinthians 4:6? What part of humanity does Paul relate darkness to? Read Luke 11:34-36; John 3:19; Romans 1:21; and Ephesians 4:18. What do these say about the nature of "darkness?"

What is the "light" in verse 6?

How do we *get* the light of the knowledge of the glory of God in the face of Jesus Christ?

God gives us the "knowledge" of what?

If God's glory is the display of his attributes and character, then how is his glory seen "in the face of Jesus Christ?" More specifically (and a little deeper), how is God's love *and* holiness seen in the person and work of Jesus?

In verse seven, Paul refers to the gospel as "this treasure in jars of clay?" What images come to your mind when you think about a jar of clay or a clay pot? What is the reasoning, in verse 7), that Paul gives for equating jars of clay with broken, sinful believers?

Read verse 7 again and then read 2 Corinthians 12:9. Why should we "boast" of our weaknesses?

DIGGING DEEPER

- Other Scripture passages on the glory of God include Exodus 24:16; 1 Chronicles 16:24; Psalm 19:1; 24:7; 86:12; 96:3; 145:5; John 13:31; 17:1; Isaiah 4:2; 6:3; 48:11; Luke 2:14; John 1:14; Ephesians 3:16; Philippians 3:21; Colossians 3:4; 2 Thessalonians 1:10; 1 Peter 4:11; and Revelation 21:23.
- One of the battle cries of the Protestant Reformation was *Soli Deo Gloria*, to God alone be the glory! They wanted to see a fundamental shift in the theology, worship, and church government from a focus on man to a focus on God. All of life is to be for the glory of God alone, not man.
- Paul writes in Romans 1:23, that sinful man "exchanged the glory of the immortal God for images resembling mortal man." How would a person "exchange" God's glory for idols?
- See also Christopher W. Morgan and Robert A. Peterson, Eds., *The Glory of God* (Wheaton: Crossway, 2010) and John Piper, *God's Passion for His Glory: Living the Vision of Jonathan Edwards* (Wheaton: Crossway, 1998).

❊ 13 ❊

God is Unchanging

SCRIPTURE MEDITATION

Of old you laid the foundation of the earth, and the heavens are the work of your hands. They will perish, but you will remain; they will all wear out like a garment. You will change them like a robe, and they will pass away, but you are the same, and your years have no end.

Psalm 102:25-27

PRAYER

Heavenly Father, you are the great I AM, the unchanging Rock on which my salvation depends. Though I change daily in my attitudes, ambitions, and character, you never change. You remain constant because you are perfect. I ask that you would guide my meditations and thoughts to the waters of your unchanging character. Would you help me see that you are dependable, constant, and true. Grant me grace as I study this attribute. I pray this in Jesus' name. Amen.

JN BIBLICAL PERSPECTIVE

God doesn't change. He remains the same—"yesterday, today, and forever" (Heb. 13:8). Christians affirm that God is *immutable*, which means that he is not subject to change in his being, attributes, or will. In other words, God never ceases to be God. He is perfect and he cannot be improved or evolve into something greater. It also means that he cannot *de*volve into something lesser.

Because God is eternal (Deut. 33:27; Rev. 1:8), all of his attributes are also eternal. That means that his power is unchanging. His sovereign control never diminishes. His steadfast love never lets go. His holiness remains unshakably pure. He is eternally wise—knowing the end from the beginning. His attributes are unchanging because *God* is unchanging.

James 1:17 states, "Every good gift and every perfect gift is from above, coming down from the Father of lights with whom there is no variation or shadow due to change." As the earth revolves around the sun, shadows change because the direction of the light changes. But there is no "shadow due to change" because the source, God, doesn't change.

Likewise, God's will, determinations, and decrees do not change. God chose us "before the foundation of the world... according to the purpose of his will" (Eph. 1:4, 5). God's "eternal purpose" has been realized in Christ Jesus (Eph. 3:11). God doesn't change his mind or think twice about doing something. Because he is all-knowing, all-wise, and all-powerful, he always acts intentionally and perfectly—no more, no less, no exceptions.

As we grow in our knowledge of the character of God, *we* are changed, transformed by the renewing of our minds (Rom. 12:2). R. C. Sproul explains,

> When our understanding of God changes, it is not because God has changed. We are the ones who change. God doesn't grow. God doesn't improve with age. God is the Lord everlasting.[10]

God has existed, from eternity past, as one God in three Persons. God the Father, God the Son, and God the Holy Spirit are all co-eternal, of the same nature and divine essence (Heb. 1:1-3). The attributes that may be attributed to the Father are also attributed to the Son and *vice versa*. Jesus manifested the fullness of God (Col. 2:9) and is therefore just as sovereign, powerful, and eternal as the Father and the Holy Spirit. Indeed, the very name that God decided to call himself—I AM WHO I AM (Ex. 3:14)—reflects the absolute immutability of God's nature.

As jobs come and go, as relationships grow and dwindle, and as our faith changes from weak to strong, you can rest in the truth of God's immutability. He doesn't change. "The LORD is my rock and my fortress" (Ps. 18:2). He doesn't waver in his promises, falter in his love, or lack surety in his plans for you. As the Psalmist expressed, "He who dwells in the shelter of the Most High will abide in the shadow of the Almighty" (Ps. 91:1). The "shadow" of God will never move. You can find rest and assurance in the shelter of the Most High because it's a shelter that will never crumble or fail.

REFLECTION QUESTIONS

In our passage, the Psalmist links God's creation to his immutability. How do you think these two things are related?

In verse 27, the Psalmist relates God's immutability with his years having "no end." What is the relationship between these two?

How might knowing the truth that God is immutable bring you comfort?

How might knowing the truth that God is immutable affect your prayer life?

Could you *trust* a God who constantly changed, grew in knowledge, or evolved into something greater? Why not?

If God's purpose, decrees, and will are eternal and unchanging, was Jesus' death on the cross "Plan B?" Read Isaiah 53:10 and Acts 2:22-24.

*D*IGGING DEEPER

- Some other Scripture passages on the immutability of God include Numbers 23:19, 20; Deuteronomy 32:4; 1 Samuel 15:29; Psalm 18:2; 33:11; 93:2; Jeremiah 31:3; Malachi 3:6; John 13:1; Romans 11:29; Ephesians 1:4-10; 3:11; Hebrews 6:17; James 1:17; and Revelation 1:8.
- Skeptics point to passages in the Bible that speak of God changing his mind or repenting (cf. Gen. 6:6; Ex. 32:14). However, many other passages are clear that he *doesn't* change his mind (cf. Num. 23:19; 1 Sam. 15:29; Ps. 33:11; Heb. 6:17). There are many places in Scripture where the writers used what has been called "phenomenological language"—which describes events as they *appear* to the observer (e.g. God's "hand," "eyes," "waking up," etc.).

God "changing his mind" is how it appeared to Moses' finite and limited knowledge.

- Another question that is often asked is, "If Jesus is God and Jesus died, did God die?" The answer is that Jesus was fully God and fully man. His *human* nature died, while his *divine* nature can never die or change (cf. Heb. 13:8). Likewise, Scripture teaches that Jesus increased in wisdom and in years (Lk. 2:52). In his human nature, Jesus grew in wisdom and had birthdays, like you and me. But he was fully God *and* fully man.
- See also Philip Graham Ryken, *Discovering God in Stories of the Bible* (Phillipsburg: P&R Publishing, 2010) and Arthur W. Pink, *The Attributes of God* (Grand Rapids: Baker Book House, 1975).

❋ 14 ❋

God is All-Knowing

SCRIPTURE MEDITATION

O LORD, you have searched me and known me! You know when I sit down and when I rise up; you discern my thoughts from afar. You search out my path and my lying down and are acquainted with all my ways. Even before a word is on my tongue, behold, O LORD, you know it altogether. You hem me in, behind and before, and lay your hand upon me. Such knowledge is too wonderful for me; it is high; I cannot attain it.

Psalm 139:1-6

PRAYER

Heavenly Father, I echo the prayer of this Psalm. You know everything about me. You know all that I have done and all that I will do. I praise you because you are all-knowing and that you have ordained all things according to your wise, powerful, and intimate knowledge of your creation. As I take this time and meditate upon your Word and upon your infinite and intimate knowledge, would you fill me with greater humility and greater love for you. I pray this in Jesus' name. Amen.

*I*N BIBLICAL PERSPECTIVE

God is *omniscient*, which means that he is all-knowing. There is not one thought, one word, or one deed that dodges the knowledge of God. God knows all past events, present events, and future events. And he doesn't just know *about* them. He knows their every detail because his knowledge is tied to him being sovereign and Creator.

God knows all that happens because he is in control of all that happens (Is. 46:8-11). However, as we noted when we meditated on his sovereignty, this control doesn't make us mere robots. We have responsibility under the sovereign control and power of God. But he knows our thoughts even before we think them. He knows our actions before we lift a finger. "Even the hairs of your head are all numbered" (Matt. 10:30). He knew that you would be reading this right now. God knows all that will happen because the future is completely dependent upon his sovereign will and purpose (Eph. 1:7-10).

His knowledge is also tied to the fact that he has created all things. Because he is the Author of life and Creator of the universe, he is perfectly acquainted with his creation. All things were created by him and for his glory. That is why you were created—to glorify him and to enjoy him forever.[11] As a potter is well acquainted with his clay, so also God is well acquainted with his creation (Rom. 9:20-23).

God knew that Adam would sin in the Garden of Eden and he knew that his only Son would suffer and die for his bride (Eph. 5:25). As Luke writes, "This Jesus, delivered up according to the definite plan and foreknowledge of God, you crucified and killed by the hands of lawless men" (Acts 2:23). In God's eternal knowledge, Jesus was slain—as it were—from "before the foundation of the world" (Rev. 13:8).

Jesus, as the full embodiment of God, also knew all things. After Jesus' resurrection from the dead, Peter proclaims to him, "Lord, you know everything" (Jn. 21:17). As the "wisdom of God" (1 Cor. 1:24), Jesus becomes *our* wisdom by faith in his life, death, and resurrection for salvation (1 Cor. 1:30). Paul writes that in Christ, "are hidden all the treasures of wisdom and knowledge" (Col. 2:3).

The Bible also speaks of God knowing his elect intimately, which is called "*fore*knowledge." It should be clear that God does not merely look down the corridor of time and know who will believe in him. While that is certainly true—and part of his omniscience—he knows who will believe because he has predestined them to believe. Again, the apostle Paul explains: "For those whom he foreknew he also predestined to be conformed to the image of his Son" (Rom. 8:29). Peter writes that believers are "elect...according to the foreknowledge of God" (1 Pet. 1:1, 2). Paul teaches in 1 Corinthians 8:3, "If anyone loves God, he is known by God" and in 2 Timothy 2:19, "The Lord knows those who are his."

God's knowledge for his people, the children of God, is saving, intimate, and comprehensive. God tells Jeremiah, "Before I formed you in the womb I knew you" (Jer. 1:5). Conversely, Jesus tells certain people who were pretending to be Christians, "I never knew you; depart from me, you workers of lawlessness" (Matt.

7:23). Jesus is the Good Shepherd, who said, "I know my own and my own know me" (Jn. 10:14).

Indeed, God knows everything. Nothing happens outside the knowledge of God. As the Old Testament writers looked ahead to the coming Messiah, the Lord Jesus Christ, they were carried along by the Holy Spirit (2 Pet. 1:21), who had complete and perfect knowledge of all the details surrounding the coming of Christ. These prophecies could only be given by One who was all-knowing.

May we join in the heavenly chorus of praise as we echo back to God his Word from Romans 11:33: "Oh, the depth of the riches and wisdom and knowledge of God!" Would we strive to "know Christ" (Phil. 3:10) and may our "love abound more and more, with knowledge" (Phil. 1:9). May you "grow in the grace and knowledge of our Lord and Savior Jesus Christ. To him be the glory both now and to the day of eternity. Amen" (2 Pet. 3:18).

*R*EFLECTION QUESTIONS

As you reflect now on Psalm 139:1-6, can you think of any secret sin you might have thought God didn't know about?

King David knew his God and his God knew him. He was a man after God's own heart (1 Sam. 13:14). In what ways can you praise God for knowing you intimately?

How might God's full knowledge of you—your sins, your struggles, your gifts, and your weaknesses—fill you with both fear and comfort?

In verse 2, David prays, "You discern my thoughts." Discerning is a knowledge of both the content of your thoughts as well as the motives behind them. How have your thoughts been lately? Have you tried to "take every thought captive to obey Christ" (2 Cor. 10:5)?

In verse 6, David expresses the fact that he "cannot attain" the "high" knowledge of God. Yet this was the temptation of Satan to Adam and Eve in the Garden of Eden (Gen. 3:5)—to attain the knowledge of God. How might you (in subtle ways) have boasted or have been prideful of your own knowledge before others—while not acknowledging how limited your knowledge really is, especially when compared to the knowledge of God? Take a few moments just search your heart and repent of this pride in specific areas.

$\mathcal{D}$IGGING DEEPER

- Some other Scripture passages on God's omniscience include Job 23:10; Psalm 90:8; 103:14; 139:23, 24; 147:5; Proverbs 19:21; Isaiah 46:8-11; Jeremiah 1:5; Ezekiel 11:5; Daniel 2:22; Hosea 7:2; Amos 3:2; John 21:17; Acts 2:23; 15:18; Romans 8:29, 30; 11:33-36 and 1 Peter 1:2.

- If God didn't know all things, could he make any promises? Could you trust him? The absolute and perfect knowledge of God should be a core belief and yet it is one we do not ponder enough. Try to make your meditations on God's knowledge applicable to where you are right now in your life.

- See also John M. Frame, *The Doctrine of the Knowledge of God* (Phillipsburg: P&R Publishing, 1987) and Edward A. Dowey, *The Knowledge of God in Calvin's Theology* (Grand Rapids: Wm. B. Eerdmans Publishing Company, 1994).

God is Everywhere

SCRIPTURE MEDITATION

Am I a God at hand, declares the LORD, and not a God afar off?
Can a man hide himself in secret places so that I cannot see him?
declares the LORD. Do I not fill heaven and earth? declares the
LORD.

Jeremiah 23:23, 24

PRAYER

Heavenly Father, I know that you are with me even now as I pray.
You are *Immanuel*—God with us. You are my eternal God and
you are everywhere right now in all of your fullness and majesty.
You fill all time and space and yet you are not bound by time and
space. As I turn now to meditate upon your character, would you
gently remind me of your sovereignty, your goodness, and your

love. Would you quiet my heart so that I would be still and know that you are God. I pray this in Jesus' name. Amen.

$\mathcal{I}$N BIBLICAL PERSEPCTIVE

God is an infinite Spirit (Jn. 4:24) who is present everywhere at all times. The universe is full of his divine presence (cf. Is. 6:3), an attribute called *omnipresence*. He dwells in all of his creation, but is not bound in any way by his creation: "Behold, heaven and the highest heaven cannot contain you" (1 Kings 8:27). In addition, wherever he is present, he is *all there* in his fullness. He does not exist more in Atlanta and less in Chicago. He is equally present everywhere.

King David prayed, "Where shall I go from your Spirit? Or where shall I flee from your presence?" (Ps. 139:7). We cannot escape the presence of God. For the Christian, this is a sweet and comforting thought; he is with us everywhere. But for the unbeliever, this is a terrible and dreadful reality. The unbeliever cannot hide from the sovereign presence and knowledge of God.

While God is everywhere in his creation, he is nevertheless *distinct* from his creation. In other words, he does not have the same substance as a tree or a rock. His nature and being are altogether distinct and different from the created world. God is both *transcendent* over all his creation (meaning that he is not subject to its confines and limitations) and he is *immanent* in all of his creation (meaning that he is fully present in his creation).

However, God is not equally present *in the same sense* in all his creation. The way in which he is "with" his chosen people, for example, is different than the way he is "with" the unbeliever. Unlike the unbeliever, the Christian is a "temple of the Holy

Spirit" (1 Cor. 6:19). God himself is "in" a believer in an entirely different way than he is "in" anything else (cf. Jn. 17:20-26). As Louis Berkhof explains, "There is an endless variety in the manner in which He is immanent in His creatures."[12]

One of the greatest truths of the gospel is that God is *with* us. Isaiah prophesied of the coming of Jesus when he wrote, "Therefore the LORD himself will give you a son. Behold, the virgin shall conceive and bear a son, and shall call his name Immanuel" (Is. 7:14; cf. Matt. 1:23). Immanuel, in Hebrew, means "God with us" (Is. 7:10). David acknowledged the God-with-us presence of the Lord, even in the face of suffering: "Even though I walk through the valley of the shadow of death, I will fear no evil, for you are with me" (Ps. 23:4). At Jesus' ascension up into heaven, following his resurrection, he told his disciples, "And behold, I am with you always, to the end of the age" (Matt. 28:20). If you have placed your trust in Jesus Christ as your Savior and Lord, God is *with you* right now.

God is everywhere. But the fullness of his being and character has stepped into the brokenness and misery of this world in the form of a little child. That child grew up and lived a perfect life without sin, to be the unblemished Lamb of God—slain to take away the sins of the world. God is with us in his Son, Jesus. May you be drawn into greater fellowship with God and may your affections be kindled for the God who is everywhere and who is with you. And may God take up residence in your heart as "Christ in you, the hope of glory" (Col. 1:27).

REFLECTION QUESTIONS

In Jeremiah 23:23, God asks a rhetorical question. What do you think the obvious answer is and why is it asked in a rhetorical way—expecting the obvious answer?

Do you find it hard to believe sometimes that God is "at hand" and not "far off?"

Meditate on the last part over verse 24: "Do I not fill heaven and earth? declares the LORD." What in this statement do you find profound and amazing? Re-phrase this statement in your own words.

How might the truth that God is everywhere be a terrifying reality to the unbeliever?

How might the truth that God is everywhere by a comforting reality to the Christian?

Theologically speaking, how is it possible for us, who are sinful, to be *with* God, who is holy? How does the life and death of Jesus relate to this cosmic problem?

*D*IGGING DEEPER

- Other Scripture passages that speak of God being everywhere include 1 Kings 8:27; Psalm 23:4; 139:7-10; 145:18; Isaiah 7:14, 10; 66:1; Matthew 28:20; John 4:24; Acts 17:27, 28; and Hebrews 4:14-16; 12:22-24.

- God's transcendence also bears the understanding that he is a divine Spirit (Jn. 4:24). The *Westminster Shorter Catechism*, Question #4 asks, "What is God?" Answer: "God is a spirit, infinite, eternal, and unchangeable, in his being, wisdom, power, holiness, justice, goodness, and truth." While he is everywhere, he is above all things because his being is distinct from his creation. He is "high and lifted up" (Is. 6:1).

- See also D. A. Carson, *The God Who is There: Finding Your Place in God's Story* (Grand Rapids: Baker Books, 2010),

Ann Spangler, *Praying the Names of God: A Daily Guide* (Grand Rapids: Zondervan, 2004) and Carol J. Ruvolo, *God With Us: Light From the Gospels* (Phillipsburg: P&R Publishing, 1998).

Notes

1. Martin Luther, *The Bondage of the Will* (Lafayette, IN: Sovereign Grace Publishers, 2001), 22.

2. J. I. Packer, *Concise Theology: A Guide to Historic Christian Beliefs* (Carol Stream, Illinois: Tyndale House Publishers, 1993), 33.

3. A. W. Pink, *The Attributes of God* (Grand Rapids: Baker Book House, 1975), 41.

4. The book of James might also be included in biblical wisdom literature.

5. Called the Septuagint (LXX). This was a translation of the Hebrew Scriptures completed in 132 B.C.

6. See John Calvin, *Institutes of the Christian Religion*, Trans. Henry Beveridge (Grand Rapids: Wm. B. Eerdmans Publishing Company, 1989), 97.

7. Pink, *The Attributes of God*, 66.

8. Historically, theologians have distinguished three "uses" of the law of God. First, the law restrains evil and sin. Second, the law shows us the depths of our sin. Third, the law reveals to us what pleases God.

9. Louis Berkhof, *Systematic Theology* (Grand Rapids: Eerdmans Publishing Company, 1938), 76.

10. R. C. Sproul, *The Character of God: Discovering the God Who Is* (Ventura, California: Regal, 1995), 84.

11. This is the answer to the *Westminster Shorter Catechism's* Question #1: "What is the chief end of man?"

12. Berkhof, *Systematic Theology*, 61.

Bibliography

Beisner, Calvin E. *Psalms of Promise: Celebrating the Majesty and Faithfulness of God*. Phillipsburg: P&R Publishing, 1994.

Berkhof, Louis. *A Summary of Christian Doctrine*. Edinburgh: Banner of Truth Trust, 2005.

_____. *Systematic Theology*. Eerdmans Publishing Company, 1938.

Bray, Gerald. *The Doctrine of God*. Downers Grove: InterVarsity Press, 1993.

Bridges, Jerry. *The Discipline of Grace: God's Role and Our Role in the Pursuit of Holiness*. Colorado Springs: NavPress, 2006.

Carson, D. A. *The God Who is There: Finding Your Place in God's Story*. Grand Rapids: Baker Books, 2010.

Charnock, Stephen. *The Existence and Attributes of God*. Grand Rapids: Baker Books, 1996.

Dowey, Edward A. *The Knowledge of God in Calvin's Theology.* Grand Rapids: Wm. B. Eerdmans Publishing Company, 1994.

Ferguson, Sinclair. *By Grace Alone: How the Grace of God Amazes Me.* Lake Mary, Florida: Reformation Trust Publishing, 2010.

Frame, John M. *The Doctrine of the Knowledge of God.* Phillipsburg: P&R Publishing, 1987.

Futato, Mark David. *Creation: A Witness to the Wonder of God.* Phillipsburg: P&R Publishing, 2000.

Keller, Timothy. *Generous Justice: How God's Grace Makes Us Just.* New York: Dutton, 2010.

Morgan, Christopher W. and Robert A. Peterson, Eds. *The Glory of God.* Wheaton: Crossway, 2010.

Packer, J. I. *Concise Theology: A Guide to Historic Christian Beliefs.* Carol Stream, Illinois: Tyndale House Publishers, 1993.

_____. *Knowing God.* Downers Grove: IVP Books, 1993.

Parsons, Burk, ed. *Assured by God: Living in the Fullness of God's Grace.* Phillipsburg: P&R Publishing, 2006.

Pink, A. W. *The Attributes of God.* Grand Rapids: Baker Book House, 1975.

_____. *The Sovereignty of God.* Edinburgh: Banner of Truth Trust, 2009).

Piper, John. *God's Passion for His Glory: Living the Vision of Jonathan Edwards*. Wheaton: Crossway, 1998.

_____. *Think: The Life of the Mind and the Love of God*. Wheaton: Crossway, 2010.

Powlison, David. *God's Love: Better Than Unconditional*. Phillipsburg: P&R Publishing, 2001.

Ruvolo, Carol J. *God With Us: Light From the Gospels*. Phillipsburg: P&R Publishing, 1998.

Ryken, Philip Graham. *Discovering God in Stories of the Bible*. Phillipsburg: P&R Publishing, 2010.

Spangler, Ann. *Praying the Names of God: A Daily Guide*. Grand Rapids: Zondervan, 2004.

Sproul, R. C. *The Character of God: Discovering the God Who Is*. Ventua, California: Regal, 1995.

_____. *The Holiness of God*. Carol Stream, Illinois: Tyndale House Publishers, 2000.

Spurgeon, Charles. *Grace: God's Unmerited Favor*. New Kensington, Pennsylvania: Whitaker House, 1996.

Wiersbe, Warren W. *Be Wise: Discern the Difference Between Man's Knowledge and God's Wisdom*. Colorado Springs: David Cook, 2010.